Vegetarian Cook
Delicious Meatless Brea
and Dinner Recipes from Bulgaria

by **Vesela Tabakova**

Table Of Contents

Favorite Vegetarian Recipes from Bulgaria

Bulgarian cuisine is a unique and delicious blend of Balkan and Mediterranean ingredients and flavors. It is healthy, nutritious and really tasty. Cooking traditions are centuries old and a lot of the dishes are prepared according to recipes handed down from generation to generation over the years. In Bulgaria food is still cooked with fresh, natural products that are slowly prepared on low heat.

The mouth-watering aromas of Bulgarian traditional dishes can evoke both the outdoor life during long hot summers and the domestic coziness of crisp, cold winters. In this book I would like to share my family's favorite non-meat dishes. I call them “non-meat” rather than vegetarian because we enjoy meat and fish, too, and I will soon be sharing more recipes with you. We simply love our fresh vegetables, which are plentiful in spring, summer and autumn, along with creamy, tangy yogurt and soft-textured but strong-flavored feta cheese (feta). In winter, as well as frozen and dried vegetables, beans, lentils and savory pastries come into their own.

For me, Bulgarian food is simply addictive –if you've tried it, you know what I mean. It might be quite different to what you usually eat at home but it is tasty, healthy and definitely worth trying.

Salads and Appetizers

Shopska Salad

Serves 5-6

Ingredients:

2-3 tomatoes, diced

1 large cucumber, peeled and diced

1-2 fresh green peppers, cut

1 onion, chopped

6 oz feta cheese, grated or crumbled

for the dressing:

3 tbsp red wine vinegar

3 tbsp sunflower or olive oil

salt, to taste

To serve: 2-3 tablespoons of finely cut parsley

Directions:

Cut the peppers into small strips and add the diced tomatoes, cucumbers and onion. Add salt, oil, vinegar and mix.

Serve topped with chopped parsley and grated feta cheese.

Snow White Salad

Serves 4

Ingredients:

1 large or two small cucumbers -fresh or pickled

4 cups of plain yogurt

½ cup of crushed walnuts

2-3 cloves garlic, crushed

½ bunch of dill

3 tbsp sunflower oil

salt, to taste

Directions:

Strain the yogurt in a piece of cheesecloth or a clean white dishtowel. You can suspend it over a bowl or the sink.

Peel and dice the cucumbers, place in a large bowl. Add the crushed walnuts and the crushed garlic, the oil and the finely chopped dill. Scoop the drained yogurt into the bowl and stir well.

Add salt to the taste, cover with cling film, and put in the fridge for at least an hour so the flavors can mix well.

Green Salad

Serves 4

Ingredients:

one head of green lettuce, washed and drained

1 cucumber, sliced

a bunch of radishes, sliced

a bunch of spring onions, finely cut

the juice of half a lemon or 2 tbsp of white wine vinegar

3 tbsp sunflower or olive oil

salt, to taste

Directions:

Cut the lettuce into thin strips. Slice the cucumber and the radishes as thinly as possible and chop the spring onions.

Mix all the salad ingredients in a large salad bowl; add the lemon juice and oil and season with salt to taste.

Roasted Eggplant and Pepper Dip

Serves 4

Ingredients:

2 medium eggplants

2 red or green bell peppers

2 tomatoes

3 cloves garlic, crushed

fresh parsley

1-2 tbsp red wine vinegar

olive oil, as needed

salt, pepper

Directions:

Wash and dry the vegetables. Prick the skin of the eggplants. Bake the eggplants, tomatoes and peppers in a pre-heated oven at 480 F for about 40 minutes, until the skins are pretty burnt. Take out of the oven and leave in a covered container for about 10 minutes.

Peel the skins off and drain well the extra juices. De-seed the peppers. Cut all the vegetables into small pieces. Add the garlic and mix well with a fork or in a food processor.

Add the olive oil, vinegar and salt to taste. Stir again. Serve cold and sprinkled with parsley.

Russian Salad

Serves 5-6

Ingredients:

3 potatoes

2 carrots

1 cup green peas, cooked, drained

1 cup mayonnaise

5-6 pickled gherkins, chopped

salt, to taste

6-7 black olives, to serve

Directions:

Boil the potatoes and carrots, then chop into small cubes. Put everything, except for the mayonnaise, in a serving bowl and mix. Add salt to taste, then stir in the mayonnaise.

Garnish with parsley and olives. Serve cold.

Fried Zucchinis with Yogurt Sauce

Serves 4

Ingredients:

4 zucchinis medium size

1 ½ cup yogurt

3 cloves garlic, crushed

a bunch of fresh dill, chopped

1 cup all purpose flour

salt, to taste

Directions:

Start by combining the garlic and chopped dill with the yogurt in a bowl. Add salt to taste and put in the fridge.

Wash and peel the zucchinis, and cut them in thin diagonal slices or in rings 0.20 inch thick. Salt and leave them in a suitable bowl placing it inclined to drain away the juices.

Coat the zucchinis with flour, then fry turning on both sides until they are golden-brown (about 3 minutes on each side). Transfer to paper towels and pat dry. Serve the zucchinis hot or cold, with garlic yogurt on the side.

Lyutenitsa-Bulgarian Tomato Dip

Serves 10

Ingredients:

5 lbs red peppers

4 lbs roma tomatoes

3 lb eggplant

2 lb carrots

6-7 garlic cloves, pressed

1/3 cup sugar

3-4 tsp salt

2/3 cup sunflower oil

Black pepper (optional)

Wash and roast the eggplants and peppers in a pre-heated oven at 480 F until the skins are pretty burnt. Take out of the oven and leave in a covered container for about 5 minutes. Peel the skins off and drain well the extra juices. Blend in a blender.

Wash the tomatoes well, cut and blend on the lower setting of a blender until they are still chunky, but not too much.

Boil the carrots.

Combine all vegetables in a large pot. Add in garlic, sugar, salt and oil and boil, stirring often, on medium-high heat for about 3-4 hours or until the liquid evaporates and the lyutenitsa thickens. You can also use the oven and bake the lyutenitsa in it.

Check whether the lyutenitsa is done by putting a spoonful on a clean, dry plate - if there is a large "watery ring" around the thicker mixture, it's not done yet.

When done, ladle into hot jars. Flip upside down or process 10 minutes in boiling water.

Potato Salad

Serves 5-6

Ingredients:

4-5 large potatoes

2-3 spring onions, finely chopped

juice of ½ a lemon

5 tbsp sunflower or olive oil

salt and pepper, to taste

fresh parsley

Directions:

Peel and boil the potatoes for about 20-25 minutes, drain and leave to cool.

In a salad bowl add the finely chopped spring onions, the lemon juice, salt, pepper and olive oil, and mix gently. Cut the potatoes into cubes and add to the salad bowl. Gently mix, sprinkle with parsley. Serve cold.

Garlic Dip

Serves 4

Ingredients:

2 potatoes

6-7 garlic cloves, finely chopped

1 cup finely chopped walnuts

½ cup extra virgin olive oil

1/4 cup red wine vinegar

Directions:

Combine boiled and peeled potatoes, chopped garlic, walnuts and salt in a blender. Puree for 30 seconds until everything is well blended. Slowly pour in oil and vinegar, alternating between them.

Continue pureeing for about 3 minutes until mixture is a smooth paste a little looser than mashed potatoes in texture.

White Bean Salad

Serves 4-5

Ingredients:

1 cup white beans

1 onion

3 tbsp white vinegar

a bunch of fresh parsley

salt and black pepper

Directions:

Wash the beans and soak them in cold water to swell overnight. Cook in the same water with the peeled onion. When tender, drain and put into a deeper bowl. Remove the onion.

Mix well oil, vinegar, salt and pepper. Pour over still warm beans, leave to cool about 30-40 minutes.

Chop the onion and the parsley, add to the beans, mix and leave to cool for at least 40 minutes. Serve cold.

Cabbage Salad

Serves 4

Ingredients:

7 oz fresh white cabbage, shredded

7 oz carrots, shredded

7 oz white turnips, shredded

½ a bunch of parsley

2 tbsp white vinegar

3 tbsp sunflower oil

salt

Directions:

Combine first three ingredients- you'll need in a large bowl - and mix well. Add the salt, vinegar and oil.

Stir and sprinkle with parsley.

Cheese Stuffed Tomatoes

Serves 4

Ingredients:

4 large tomatoes

9 oz feta cheese, crumbled

1 tsp paprika

Directions:

Cut the top of each tomato in such a way as to be able to stuff the tomato and cover with the cap. Scoop out the seeds and central part of the tomatoes to create a hollow.

Mash the scooped out parts of the tomatoes, add to the feta cheese and stir to make a homogeneous mixture. Add paprika.

Stuff the tomatoes with the mixture and cover with the caps. Serve chilled, garnished with sprays of parsley.

Roasted Peppers with Garlic and Parsley

Serves 4-6

Ingredients:

2 lb red and green bell peppers

4-5 tbsp sunflower oil

4 tbsp white vinegar

3-4 cloves garlic, chopped

a small bunch of fresh parsley

salt and pepper

Directions:

Grill the peppers or roast them in the oven at 480 F until the skins are a little burnt. Place the roasted peppers in a brown paper bag or a lidded container and leave covered for about 10 minutes. This makes it easier to peel them. Peel the skins and remove the seeds.

Cut the peppers into 1 inch strips lengthwise and layer them in a bowl. Mix together the oil, vinegar, salt and pepper, chopped garlic and the chopped parsley leaves. Pour over the peppers. Cover the roasted peppers and chill for an hour.

Shepherds' Salad

Serves 6

Ingredients:

5-6 tomatoes, diced

2 cucumbers, sliced

½ cup mushrooms, sliced

2 red peppers, sliced

1 onion, chopped

4 eggs, boiled and sliced

9 oz feta cheese, grated

½ bunch parsley, finely cut

4 tbsp olive oil

1 tbsp vinegar

1 tsp salt

20-30 black olives

Directions:

Dice the tomatoes and cut the cucumber and peppers. Chop the onion and thinly slice the mushrooms.

Combine all ingredients in a salad bowl. Drizzle with olive oil and vinegar, add salt and mix well.

Split the salad in 6 plates and sprinkle with feta cheese and finely chopped parsley. Boil the eggs for 10 minutes, then cut them in discs. Garnish the salads with egg slices and olives. Serve chilled.

Bulgarian Spinach Salad

Serves 4

Ingredients:

1 bag baby spinach, washed and dried

4-5 spring onions, finely chopped

1 cucumber, cut

1/2 cup walnuts, halved

2/3 cup yogurt

3 tbsp red wine vinegar

4 tbsp olive oil

salt and freshly ground black pepper, to taste

Directions:

Prepare the dressing by blending yogurt, olive oil and vinegar in a cup.

Place the spinach leaves in a large salad bowl, together with the onions, cucumber and walnuts.

Season to taste with black pepper and salt, stir well, and toss with the dressing.

Okra Salad

Serves 4

Ingredients:

1.2 lb young okras

1 lemon

½ bunch parsley, chopped

2 hard tomatoes

¼ cup oil

½ tsp black pepper

salt

Directions:

Trim okras, wash and cook in salted water. Drain and cool when tender.

In a small bowl mix well the lemon juice and oil, salt and pepper. Pour over okras arranged in a bowl and sprinkle with chopped parsley.

Wash tomatoes and cut them into slices, then garnish the salad with them.

Cucumber Salad

Serves 4

Ingredients:

2 medium cucumbers, sliced

a bunch of fresh dill, finely cut

2 cloves garlic

3 tbsp apple vinegar

5 tbsp olive oil

salt, to taste

Directions:

Cut the cucumbers in rings and put them in a salad bowl. Add the finely cut dill, the pressed garlic and season with salt, vinegar and oil.

Mix well and serve cold.

Soups

Monastery Style White Bean Soup

Serves 6

Ingredients:

1 cup dry white beans

2-3 carrots

2 onions, finely chopped

1-2 tomatoes, grated

1 red bell pepper, chopped

4 -5 springs of fresh mint and parsley

1 tsp paprika

5 tbsp sunflower oil

salt, to taste

Directions:

Soak the beans in cold water for 3-4 hours, drain and discard the water. Cover the beans with cold water again.

Add the oil, finely chopped carrots, onions and pepper. Bring to the boil and simmer until the beans are tender. Add the grated tomatoes, mint, paprika and salt. Simmer for another 15 minutes.

Serve sprinkled with finely chopped parsley.

Tarator–Bulgarian Cold Cucumber Soup

Serves 4

Ingredients:

1 large or two small cucumbers

2 cups yogurt

4-5 cloves garlic, crushed or chopped

1 cup cold water

6 tbsp sunflower or olive oil

2 bunches of fresh dill, finely chopped

½ cup crushed walnuts

Directions:

Wash the cucumber, peel and cut into very small cubes.

In a large bowl dilute the yogurt with water to taste, add the cucumber and garlic stirring well. Add salt to the taste, garnish with the dill and the crushed walnuts and put in the fridge to cool.

Spinach Soup

Serves 4

Ingredients:

14 oz frozen spinach

5.5 oz feta cheese, crumbled

1 large onion or 4-5 spring onions

2 -3 tbsp light cream

3-4 tbsp olive or sunflower oil

1/4 cup white rice

1-2 cloves garlic

black pepper

salt

Directions:

Chop the onion and spinach. Heat the oil in a cooking pot, add the onion and spinach and sauté together for a few minutes, until just softened. Add chopped garlic and rice and stir for a minute.

Remove from heat. Add about 2 cups of hot water and season with salt and pepper.

Bring back to the boil, then reduce the heat and simmer for around 30 minutes.

In the meantime crumble the cheese with a fork. When the soup is ready stir in the crumbled feta cheese and the cream. Serve hot.

Nettle Soup

Serves 4

Ingredients:

1.5 lb young top shoots of nettles, well washed

3-4 tbsp sunflower oil

2 potatoes, diced small

1 bunch spring onions, coarsely chopped

freshly boiled water

1 tsp salt

Directions:

Clean the young nettles, wash and cook them in slightly salted water. Drain, rinse, drain again and then chop or pass through a sieve.

Sauté the chopped spring onions and potatoes in the oil until the potatoes start to color a little.

Turn off the heat, add the nettles, then gradually stir in 2 cups of water. Stir well, then simmer until the potatoes are cooked through.

Thick Herb Soup

Serves 4

Ingredients:

1 bunch of parsley, finely cut

1 bunch dill, finely cut

½ bunch of mint leaves, finely cut

1 celery rib, chopped

3 tbsp olive oil

2 tbsp plain flour

3 cups. water

½ cup thick yogurt or sour cream

juice of a lemon

2 egg yolks

1 tsp salt

Directions:

Wash the herbs, remove stalks and snip or chop finely.

Heat oil in a cooking pot, add prepared herbs, cover and simmer gently. When the herbs are tender, add flour, stir well. Cook for a few moments before slowly adding the water, stirring all the time.

Simmer for about 10-15 min. Mix separately egg yolks, thick yogurt (or sour cream) and lemon juice. Add to the soup slowly, then stir well. The soup should not be allowed to boil any more.

Lentil Soup

Serves 8-9

Ingredients:

1 ½ cups brown lentils

2 onions, chopped

5 -6 cloves garlic, peeled

3 medium carrots, chopped

2 -3 medium tomatoes, ripe

4 tbsp olive oil

1 tsp paprika

1 tsp savory or oregano

Directions:

Heat the oil in a cooking pot, add the onions and carrots and sauté until golden. Add the paprika and washed lentils with 4-5 cups of warm water; continue to simmer. Chop the tomatoes and pepper and add them to the soup about 15 min after the lentils have started to simmer. Add savory and peeled garlic cloves.

Let it simmer until the lentils are soft. Salt to taste.

Tomato Soup

Serves 4

Ingredients:

4 cups chopped fresh tomatoes or 2 cups canned tomatoes

1 large onion, diced

1/2 cup vermicelli

3 cups water

2 garlic cloves, chopped

3 tbsp olive oil

1 tsp salt

½ tsp black pepper

1 tsp sugar

½ bunch fresh parsley

Directions:

Sauté onion and garlic in oil in a large soup pot. When onions have softened, add tomatoes and cook for 10 minutes.

Stir in the spices and mix well to coat vegetables. Add water and simmer for 20 minutes.

Blend the soup then return to the pot. Add in vermicelli and a teaspoon of sugar. Simmer for 10 minutes, stirring occasionally. Sprinkle with parsley and serve.

Main Dishes

Baked Beans

Serves 6

Ingredients:

1 ½ cups dried white beans

2 medium onions, chopped

1 red bell pepper, chopped

1 carrot, chopped

6 tbsp sunflower oil

1 tsp paprika

1 tsp black pepper

1 tbsp plain flour

½ bunch fresh parsley and mint

1 tsp salt

Directions:

Wash the beans and soak in water overnight. In the morning discard the water, pour enough cold water to cover the beans, add one of the onions, peeled but left whole. Cook until the beans are soft but not falling apart. If there is too much water left, drain the beans.

Chop the other onion and fry it a frying pan along with the chopped bell pepper and the carrot. Add paprika, plain flour and the beans. Stir well and pour the mixture in a baking dish along with some parsley, mint, and salt.

Bake in a preheated to 350 F oven for 20 to 30 minutes. The beans should not be too dry. Serve warm.

Rice Stuffed Bell Peppers

Serves 4

Ingredients:

8 bell peppers, cored and seeded

1 ½cups rice, washed and drained

2 onions, chopped

1 tomato, chopped

fresh parsley, chopped

3 tbsp oil

1 tbsp paprika

Directions:

Heat the oil and sauté the onions for 2-3 minutes. Add the paprika, the washed and rinsed rice, the tomato, and season with salt and pepper.

Add ½ cup of hot water and cook the rice until the water is absorbed. Stuff each pepper with the mixture using a spoon. Every pepper should be ¾ full.

Arrange the peppers in a deep oven proof dish and top up with warm water to half fill the dish. Cover and bake for about 20 minutes at 350 F.

Uncover and cook for another 15 minutes until the peppers are well cooked. Serve on their own or with plain yogurt.

Stuffed Peppers with Eggs and Feta Cheese

Serves 4

Ingredients:

8 red bell peppers

6 eggs

9 oz feta cheese

a bunch of parsley

2 cups breadcrumbs

sunflower oil

Directions:

Grill the peppers or roast them in the oven at 450 F. Peel and deseed the peppers. Mix the crumbled feta cheese with 4 beaten eggs.

Stuff the peppers with the mixture. Beat the remaining two eggs. Roll each stuffed pepper first in breadcrumbs then dip in the beaten eggs.

Fry in hot oil turning once. Serve sprinkled with parsley.

Stuffed Red Bell Peppers with White Beans

Serves: 5

Ingredients:

10 dried red peppers

1 cup dried beans

1 onion

3 cloves garlic

2 tbsp flour

1 carrot

1 bunch of parsley

½ crushed walnuts

1 tsp paprika

salt, to taste

Directions:

Put the dried peppers in warm water and leave them for 1 hour. Cook the beans. Chop the carrot and the onion, sauté them and add them to the cooked beans. Add as well the paprika, finely chopped parsley and the walnuts. Stir the mixture to make it homogeneous.

Drain the peppers, then fill them with the mixture and place in a roasting tin, covering the peppers' openings with flour to seal them during the baking. Bake it for about 30 min at 350 F

Monastery Stew

Serves 5-6

Ingredients:

3-4 potatoes, diced

2-3 tomatoes, diced

1-2 carrots, chopped

1 onion, finely chopped

1 cup small onions (shallots), whole

1 celery rib, chopped

2 cups fresh mushrooms, chopped

1 cup black olives, pitted

1/4 cup rice

1/2 cup white wine

1/4 cup sunflower oil

1 bunch of parsley

1 tsp black pepper

1 tsp salt

Directions:

Sauté the finely chopped onion, carrots and celery in a little oil. Add the shallots, olives, mushrooms and black pepper and stir well. Add the wine and one cup of water and salt.

Cover and let simmer until tender. After 15 minutes add the diced potatoes, the rice, and the tomato pieces.

Transfer everything into a clay pot, sprinkle with parsley and bake for about 30 minutes at 350 F.

Stuffed Eggplants

Serves 4

Ingredients:

4-5 eggplants

5 tomatoes, grated

4 onions, chopped

2 carrots, grated

1 celery rib, chopped

4-5 cloves garlic

half a lemon

1 bay leaf

3 tbsp breadcrumbs

a bunch of parsley

1 tbsp paprika

1/3 cup sunflower oil

1 tsp salt

Directions:

Remove the stalks from the eggplants and carefully hollow them out. Salt them and leave them aside for 30 minutes.

Sauté the chopped onions, the grated carrots and celery along with the grated tomatoes, finely chopped garlic and parsley, the bay leaf, pepper and salt. Rinse the eggplants, dry them with kitchen paper and stuff them with the mixture. Top with a slice of tomato and sprinkle with breadcrumbs. Arrange standing in a roasting tin.

Bake in a moderate oven until the eggplants are soft to the touch.

Remove from the oven and leave to cool. Serve cold, garnished with slices of lemon.

Potato and Leek Stew

Serves 4

Ingredients:

3-4 potatoes

2-3 leek stems cut into thick rings

5-6 tbsp olive oil

½ bunch of parsley

5.5 oz grated yellow cheese (cheddar or Gruyère)

salt

Directions:

Peel the potatoes, wash them and cut them into small cubes. Slice the leeks.

Put the potatoes and the leeks in a pot along with some water and the oil. The water should cover the vegetables.

Season with salt and bring to the boil then simmer until tender. Sprinkle with the finely chopped parsley and the grated yellow cheese.

Spinach with Rice

Serves 4

Ingredients:

3-4 cups fresh spinach, washed, drained and chopped

½ cup of rice

1 onion, chopped

1 carrot, chopped

¼ cup olive oil

2 cups water

Directions:

Heat the oil in a large skillet and cook the onions and the carrot until soft, add the paprika and the washed and drained rice and mix well. Add two cups of warm water stirring constantly as the rice absorbs it, and simmer for 10 more minutes.

Wash the spinach well and cut it in strips then add to the rice and cook until it wilts. Remove from the heat and season to taste. Serve with yogurt.

Feta Cheese Stuffed Zucchinis

Serves 5-6

Ingredients:

5-6 zucchinis

5.5 oz feta cheese, grated

3 eggs

1 onion, finely chopped

½ cup milk

2 oz butter

salt

Directions:

Slice the peeled zucchinis lengthwise, hollow and salt. Sauté the finely chopped onion in half of the butter. Combine half of the milk, grated feta cheese and 1 egg in a bowl.

Stuff the zucchinis with the mixture, arrange in a baking dish and pour over the remaining 2 eggs beaten with the rest of the milk.

Bake for approximately 30 min to 350 F in a preheated oven. A few minutes before the dish is ready fleck the remaining butter over the zucchinis.

Mish-Mash

Serves 5-6

Ingredients:

2 small onions, chopped

1 green bell pepper, chopped

2 red bell peppers, chopped

4 tomatoes, cubed

2 garlic cloves, crushed

8 eggs

10 oz feta cheese, crumbled

4 tbsp olive oil

half a bunch parsley

black pepper

salt

Directions:

In a large pan sauté onions over medium heat, till transparent. Reduce heat and add bell peppers and garlic. Continue cooking until soft.

Add the tomatoes and continue simmering until the mixture is almost dry. Add the cheese and all eggs and cook until well mixed and not too liquid.

Season with black pepper and remove from heat. Sprinkle with parsley.

Feta Cheese Baked In Foil

Serves 4

Ingredients:

14 oz hard feta cheese

2 oz butter

1 tbsp paprika

1 tsp savory

Directions:

Cut the feta cheese into four medium-thick slices and place on sheets of butter-lined foil.

Place cubes of butter on top each feta cheese piece, sprinkle with paprika and savory and wrap. Place in a tray and bake in a moderate oven. Serve wrapped in the foil.

Potatoes Baked in Milk

Serves 5-6

Ingredients:

4-5 medium potatoes

1 cup milk

5 tbsp olive oil

1 tsp salt

1 tsp black pepper

1 tsp paprika

1 tsp savory

Directions:

Wash the potatoes, peel them and cut them in thin 1/4 inch slices. Put in a large baking dish together with the milk, oil, salt, pepper, paprika and savory.

Mix everything very well. Bake for about 30 minutes at 350 F.

Stuffed Grapevine Leaves–Lozovi Sarmi

Serves 6

Ingredients:

1.5 lb grapevine leaves, canned

1 ½ cups rice

2 onions, chopped

2-3 cloves garlic, chopped

½ cup of currants

half bunch of parsley

half bunch of dill

1 lemon, juice only

1 tsp dried mint

1 tsp salt

1 tsp black pepper

½ cup olive oil

Directions:

Heat 3 tablespoons of olive oil in a frying pan and Sauté the onions and garlic until golden. Add the washed and drained rice, the currants, dill and parsley. Pour half a cup of olive oil and lemon juice in it. Add the black pepper, dried mint, salt and stir well.

Place leaf on a chopping board, with the stalk towards you and the vein side up. Snip away any tough remnants of the vein. Place about 1 teaspoon of the filling in the center of the leaf and towards the bottom edge. Fold the bottom part of the leaf over the filling, then draw the sides in and towards the middle, rolling the leaf up. The vine leaves should be well tucked in, forming a neat parcel. The stuffing should feel compact and evenly distributed.

Cover the bottom of a pot with grapevine leaves and stand the stuffed vine leaf parcels, packing them tightly together, on top. Pour water some water, to just below the level of the stuffed leaves. Pour ½ cup olive oil over the stuffed vine leaves, then place a small, flat oven proof dish upside down on top, in order to prevent scattering. Cover with a lid.

Bring to the boil, then reduce the heat and simmer for about an hour checking occasionally that the bottom of the pot does not burn. The liquid should be absorbed giving a lovely sticky finish to the stuffed leaves. Serve warm or cold.

Breaded Cheese

Serves 4

Ingredients:

14 oz feta cheese

2 eggs, beaten

2 tbsp flour

3-4 tbsp breadcrumbs

vegetable oil for frying

Directions:

Cut the cheese in 1/2 inch thick slices. Dip each piece first in cold water, then roll in the flour, then in the beaten eggs, and finally in the breadcrumbs.

Fry these cheese pieces in preheated oil on both sides. Serve warm.

Stewed Green Beans

Serves 5-6

Ingredients:

2.25 lb green beans, fresh or frozen

2 onions, chopped

4 cloves garlic, crushed

1 cup olive oil

1 bunch fresh parsley, chopped

1 bunch of fresh dill, finely chopped

2 potatoes, peeled and cut in small chunks

2 carrots, sliced

1 cup water

2 tsp salt

pepper to taste

Directions:

Sauté the onions and the garlic lightly in olive oil. Add the green beans, and the remaining ingredients.

Cover and simmer over medium heat for about an hour or until all vegetables are tender. Check after 30 minutes; add more water if necessary. Serve warm - sprinkled with the fresh dill.

Cabbage and Rice Stew

Serves 4

Ingredients:

1 cup long grain white rice

2 cups water

2 tbsp olive oil

1 small onion, chopped

1 clove garlic, crushed

1/4 head cabbage, cored and shredded

2 tomatoes, diced

1 tbsp paprika

½ bunch of parsley

salt to taste

black pepper to taste

Directions:

Heat the olive oil in a large pot. Add the onion and garlic and cook until transparent. Add the paprika, rice and water, stir and bring to boil. Simmer for 10 minutes.

Add the shredded cabbage, the tomatoes, and cook for about 20 minutes, stirring occasionally, until the cabbage cooks down. Season with salt and pepper and serve sprinkled with parsley.

Patatnik–Potato Pie from the Rhodope Mountains

Serves 4-5

Ingredients:

4-5 medium potatoes

2 eggs

6 oz feta cheese, crumbled

1 tsp dried mint

1 tsp salt

4 oz butter

Directions:

Peel and grate the potatoes. Add salt and set aside to drain. Crumble the feta cheese and mix it with the eggs and mint. Add the drained potatoes and stir well.

Melt the butter and put half of it in a baking dish, then pour over the potato mixture and spread it evenly. Add the rest of the butter. Bake in an oven at 350 F for about 20 min.

Panagiurishte-Style Eggs

Serves 4

Ingredients:

12 eggs

2 cups plain yogurt

12 oz feta cheese, grated

2 tsp paprika

3 cloves garlic

2 oz butter

Directions:

Crush the garlic and stir together with the yogurt and the grated cheese. Divide the mixture into four plates.

Poach the eggs, take them out with a serving spoon and place three eggs on top of the mixture in each plate.

Brown the butter together with the red pepper and pour one quarter over each plate before serving.

Stuffed Cabbage Leaves–Zelevi Sarmi

Serves 8

Ingredients:

20-30 pickled cabbage leaves

1 onion, diced

2 leek stems, chopped

1 ½ cup white rice

½ cup currants

½ cup almonds, blanched, peeled, and chopped

2 tsp paprika

1 tbsp dried peppermint

½ tsp black pepper

½ cup olive oil

salt to taste

Directions:

Sauté the onion and the leeks in the oil for about 2-3 minutes. Add the paprika, the black pepper and the washed and drained rice and continue sautéing until the rice is translucent. Remove from heat and add the currants, finely chopped almonds and the peppermint. Add salt only if the cabbage leaves are not too salty.

In a large pot place a few cabbage leaves on the base. Place a cabbage leaf on a large plate with the thickest part closest to you. Spoon 1-2 teaspoons of the rice mixture and fold over each edge to create a tight sausage-like parcel.

Place in the pot, making two or three layers of sarmi. Cover with a few cabbage leaves and pour over some boiling water so that the water level remains lower than the top layer of cabbage leaves.

Top with a small dish upside down to prevent scattering.

Bring to the boil then lower the heat and cook for around 40 minutes. Serve warm or at room temperature.

New Potatoes with Herbs

Serves 4-5

Ingredients:

2 lb small new potatoes

1 tbsp peppermint

4 tbsp olive oil

1 tbsp finely chopped parsley

1 tbsp rosemary

1 tbsp oregano

1 tbsp dill

1 tsp salt

1 tsp black pepper

Directions:

Wash the young potatoes, cut them in halves if too big, and put them in a baking dish. Add olive oil and stir the potatoes. Season with herbs, salt and pepper.

Bake for 30-40 minutes at 350 F

Banitsa-Bulgarian Cheese Pastry

Serves 8

Ingredients:

14 oz filo pastry

5 eggs

½ cup yogurt

8 oz feta cheese

3.5 oz butter

Directions:

Turn the oven to 350 F. Mix well the eggs, cheese and yogurt in a bowl. Melt the butter in a bowl.

Grease the base of a baking tray, at least 1.5 inch deep, with some of the butter. Take the filo sheets and lay them on a dry surface. Place one sheet of filo pastry in the baking tray. Brush with melted butter using a pastry brush. Lay another sheet of pastry on top and brush with butter. Sprinkle some of the cheese mixture evenly over the butter-basted pastry.

Continue alternating two sheets of butter-basted pastry with the cheese mixture. Repeat for 6 or 7 layers until all the sheets of pastry have been used up or the pie reaches the top of the baking tray, but make sure you finish with a sheet of pastry on top.

If there is any mixture left over brush the top of the banitsa in the tray, if there is none left - brush some butter. Place the tray in the oven and bake for 20 minutes until slightly risen and golden. Serve warm.

Spinach-Cheese Pastry

Serves 8

Ingredients:

14 oz filo pastry

2 cups washed fresh spinach

2 eggs

1/4 cup sour cream

1/4 cup yogurt

7 oz feta cheese, crumbled

½ cup sunflower oil

1 tsp salt

Directions:

Preheat oven to 350 F. Wash and drain the spinach then chop it and place in a big bowl. Add salt and mix. Leave for about 10 minutes and then drain the excess water. Mix together eggs, feta cheese and yogurt and add to the spinach.

Grease a baking tray, at least 1.5 inch deep. Take filo sheets and lay them on a dry surface. Place one sheet of pastry into the baking tray. Brush with oil, using a pastry brush. Place another sheet of pastry on top and brush with oil. Add some filling and spread evenly. Repeat for 6 or 7 layers until the pie reaches the top but make sure you finish with the pastry on top.

Place the banitsa in the oven, uncovered, for about 35 minutes. Take out of the oven and pour over it 1/4 cup sour cream blended with 1/4 cup of yogurt.

Return to the oven and bake for another 15 minutes until golden. Serve warm or at room temperature.

Eggs Baked in Tomato Sauce

Serves 2

Ingredients:

1 small onion, finely cut

1 garlic clove, chopped

1 red pepper, chopped

2 eggs

1 can tomatoes, diced and undrained

1/2 tsp dried oregano

1/2 tsp cumin

2 tbsp olive oil

salt and black pepper, to taste

2 tbsp grated Parmesan cheese

Directions:

In a skillet, sauté onion and pepper over medium heat, until soft. Add garlic and cook until just fragrant.

Stir in the tomatoes and bring to a boil. Crack 2 eggs into the skillet and season with, salt, pepper, oregano and cumin.

Sprinkle the cheese over the eggs and cook the for about 10 minutes, until the whites are just set. Serve with toast.

Desserts

Baked Apples

Serves 4

Ingredients:

8 medium sized apples

1/3 cup walnuts, crushed

3/4 cup sugar

3 tbsp raisins, soaked

vanilla, cinnamon according to taste

1.7 oz butter

Directions:

Peel and carefully hollow the apples. Prepare stuffing by beating butter, 3/4 cup of sugar, crushed walnuts, raisins and cinnamon.

Stuff the apples and place in an oiled dish, pour over 1-2 tbsp of water and bake in a moderate oven. Serve warm with a scoop of vanilla ice cream.

Fried Bread Slices–French Toast

Serves 4

Ingredients:

stale bread

3 eggs, beaten

1 cup milk

½ cup sunflower oil

Directions:

Slice the bread into thin ½ inch slices. Dip first in milk, then in the beaten eggs. Fry in hot oil.

Serve hot, sprinkled with sugar, honey, jam, feta cheese or whatever topping you prefer.

Pumpkin Banitsa

Serves 8

Ingredients:

14 oz filo pastry

1.5 lb pumpkin

1 cup walnuts, coarsely chopped

½ cup sugar

6 tbsp oil

1 tbsp cinnamon

10 g vanilla

Directions:

Grate the pumpkin and steam it until tender. Cool and add the walnuts, sugar, cinnamon and the vanilla.

Place a few sheets of pastry in the baking dish, sprinkle with oil and spread the filling on top. Repeat this a few times finishing with a sheet of pastry.

Bake for 20 minutes at medium heat. Let the Pumpkin Pie cool down and dust with the powder sugar.

Sweet Cheese Balls with Syrup

Serves 6

Ingredients:

5.5 oz feta or cottage cheese

3 eggs

1 cup flour

1 tsp baking soda

1 cup sunflower oil

For the syrup: 3 cups water, 3/2 cup sugar, vanilla

Directions:

Mix the feta cheese and eggs well, before gradually adding the flour, followed by the baking soda.

Shape into balls with a spoon and fry in hot oil until golden-brown.

When cooled, pour over syrup made from water, sugar and vanilla.

Bulgarian Cake

Serves 12 (24 pieces)

Ingredients:

3 eggs, beaten

1 cup sugar

1 cup yogurt

½ cup vegetable oil

1 tbsp baking powder

1 tbsp vanilla

1 tsp grated fresh lemon rind

1 tbsp cocoa

3 cups plain flour

Directions:

Beat eggs with the sugar and add the vegetable oil. Add yogurt Mix the baking powder with the flour and add to the eggs along with vanilla and lemon rind.

Preheat oven to 350 F. Warm a 10 inch tube pan in the oven. Pour two thirds of the mixture into the warm cake tin. Add a tablespoon of cocoa to the remaining dough, mix well and pour in the cake tin.

Bake for about 35 minutes.

Caramel Cream

Serves 8

Ingredients:

2 cups sugar

4 cups cold milk

8 eggs

2 tsp vanilla

Directions:

Melt 1/4 of the sugar in a non-stick pan over low heat. When the sugar has turned into caramel pour it in the 8 cup-size oven proof pots covering only the bottom.

Whisk the eggs with the rest of the sugar and the vanilla and slowly add the milk. Stir the mixture well and divide between the pots.

Place the small pots in a large, deep baking dish. Pour 3-4 cups of water into the dish. Place in an oven preheated to 280 F for about an hour. Turn the cream out on to a dessert plate.

Bulgarian Rice Pudding

Serves 4

Ingredients:

1 cup short-grain white rice

6 tbsp sugar

1 ½ cup water

1 ½ cup whole milk

1 cinnamon stick

1 strip lemon zest

Pistachios and rose petals for garnish, optional

Directions:

Place the rice in a saucepan, cover with water and cook over low heat for about 15 minutes. Add milk, sugar, cinnamon stick and lemon zest and cook over very low heat, stirring frequently until the mixture is creamy. Do not let it boil. When ready discard cinnamon stick and lemon zest.

Serve warm or at room temperature garnished with shelled pistachio halves and rose petals, if desired.

Baklava-Walnut Pie

Serves 15

Ingredients:

14 oz filo pastry

1 cup ground walnuts

1 tsp vanilla sugar

8 oz butter

For the syrup:

2 cups sugar

2 cups water

1 tbsp vanilla

2 tbsp lemon zest

Directions:

Grease a baking tray and place 2-3 sheets of pastry. Crush the walnuts and spread some evenly on the pastry. Place two more sheets of the filo pastry on top. Repeat until all the pastry sheets and walnuts have been used up. Always finish with some sheets of pastry on top.

Cut the pie in the tray into small squares. Melt the butter and pour it over the pie. Bake in a preheated oven at 350 F until light brown. When ready set aside to cool.

The syrup: Combine water and sugar in a saucepan. Add vanilla and lemon zest and bring to the boil, then lower the heat and simmer for about 5 minutes until the syrup is nearly thick. Pour hot syrup over the cold baked pie, Leave to stand for at least 1-2 days until completely dry.

FREE BONUS RECIPES: 10 Ridiculously Easy Jam and Jelly Recipes Anyone Can Make

A Different Strawberry Jam

Makes 6-7 11 oz jars

Ingredients:

4 lb fresh small strawberries (stemmed and cleaned)

5 cups sugar

1 cup water

2 tbsp lemon juice or 1 tsp citric acid

Directions:

Mix water and sugar and bring to the boil. Simmer sugar syrup for 5-6 minutes then slowly drop in the cleaned strawberries. Stir and bring to the boil again. Lower heat and simmer, stirring and skimming any foam off the top once or twice. Drop a small amount of the jam on a plate and wait a minute to see if it has thickened. If it has gelled enough, turn off the heat. If not, keep boiling and test every 5 minutes until ready. Two or three minutes before you remove the jam from the heat, add lemon juice or citric acid and stir well.

Ladle the hot jam in the jars until 1/8-inch from the top. Place the lid on top and flip the jar upside down. Continue until all of the jars are filled and upside down. Allow the jam to cool completely before turning right-side up. Press on the lid to check and see if it has sealed. If one of the jars lids doesn’t pop up- the jar is not sealed–store it in a refrigerator.

Raspberry Jam

Makes 4-5 11 oz jars

Ingredients:

4 cups raspberries

4 cups sugar

1 tsp vanilla extract

1/2 tsp citric acid

Directions:

Gently wash and drain the raspberries. Lightly crush them with a potato masher, food mill or a food processor. Do not puree, it is better to have bits of fruit. Sieve half of the raspberry pulp to remove some of the seeds. Combine sugar and raspberries in a wide, thick-bottomed pot and bring mixture to a full rolling boil, stirring constantly. Skim any scum or foam that rises to the surface. Boil until the jam sets.

Test by putting a small drop on a cold plate – if the jam is set, it will wrinkle when given a small poke with your finger. Add citric acid, vanilla, and stir. Simmer for 2-3 minutes more, then ladle into hot jars. Flip upside down or process 10 minutes in boiling water.

Raspberry-Peach Jam

Makes 4-5 11 oz jars

Ingredients:

2 lb peaches

1 1/2 cup raspberries

4 cups sugar

1 tsp citric acid

Directions:

Wash and slice the peaches. Clean the raspberries and combine them with the peaches is a wide, heavy-bottomed saucepan. Cover with sugar and set aside for a few hours or overnight. Bring the fruit and sugar to a boil over medium heat, stirring occasionally. Remove any foam that rises to the surface.

Boil until the jam sets. Add citric acid and stir. Simmer for 2-3 minutes more, then ladle into hot jars. Flip upside down or process 10 minutes in boiling water.

Blueberry Jam

Makes 4-5 11 oz jars

Ingredients:

4 cups granulated sugar

3 cups blueberries (frozen and thawed or fresh)

3/4 cup honey

2 tbsp lemon juice

1 tsp lemon zest

Directions:

Gently wash and drain the blueberries. Lightly crush them with a potato masher, food mill or a food processor. Add the honey, lemon juice, and lemon zest, then bring to a boil over medium-high heat. Boils for 10-15 minutes, stirring from time to time. Boil until the jam sets.

Test by putting a small drop on a cold plate – if the jam is set, it will wrinkle when given a small poke with your finger. Skim off any foam, then ladle the jam into jars. Seal, flip upside down or process for 10 minutes in boiling water.

Triple Berry Jam

Makes 4-5 11 oz jars

Ingredients:

1 cup strawberries

1 cup raspberries

2 cups blueberries

4 cups sugar

1 tsp citric acid

Directions:

Mix berries and add sugar. Set aside for a few hours or overnight. Bring the fruit and sugar to the boil over medium heat, stirring frequently. Remove any foam that rises to the surface. Boil until the jam sets. Add citric acid, salt and stir.

Simmer for 2-3 minutes more, then ladle into hot jars. Flip upside down or process 10 minutes in boiling water.

Red Currant Jelly

Makes 6-7 11 oz jars

Ingredients:

2 lb fresh red currants

1/2 cup water

3 cups sugar

1 tsp citric acid

Directions:

Place the currants into a large pot, and crush with a potato masher or berry crusher. Add in water, and bring to a boil. Simmer for 10 minutes. Strain the fruit through a jelly or cheese cloth and measure out 4 cups of the juice. Pour the juice into a large saucepan, and stir in the sugar. Bring to full rolling boil, then simmer for 20-30 minutes, removing any foam that may rise to the surface. When the jelly sets, ladle in hot jars, flip upside down or process in boiling water for 10 minutes.

White Cherry Jam

Makes 3-4 11 oz jars

Ingredients:

2 lb cherries

3 cups sugar

2 cups water

1 tsp citric acid

Directions:

Wash and stone cherries. Combine water and sugar and bring to the boil. Boil for 5-6 minutes then remove from heat and add cherries. Bring to a rolling boil and cook until set. Add citric acid, stir and boil 1-2 minutes more.

Ladle in hot jars, flip upside down or process in boiling water for 10 minutes.

Cherry Jam

Makes 3-4 11 oz jars

Ingredients:

2 lb fresh cherries, pitted, halved

4 cups sugar

1/2 cup lemon juice

Directions:

Place the cherries in a large saucepan. Add sugar and set aside for an hour. Add the lemon juice and place over low heat. Cook, stirring occasionally, for 10 minutes or until sugar dissolves. Increase heat to high and bring to a rolling boil.

Cook for 5-6 minutes or until jam is set. Remove from heat and ladle hot jam into jars, seal and flip upside down.

Oven Baked Ripe Figs Jam

Makes 3-4 11 oz jars

Ingredients:

2 lb ripe figs

2 cups sugar

1 ½ cups water

2 tbsp lemon juice

Directions:

Arrange the figs in a Dutch oven, if they are very big, cut them in halves. Add sugar and water and stir well. Bake at 350 F for about one and a half hours. Do not stir. You can check the readiness by dropping a drop of the syrup in a cup of cold water – if it falls to the bottom without dissolving, the jam is ready. If the drop dissolves before falling, you can bake it a little longer. Take out of the oven, add lemon juice and ladle in the warm jars. Place the lids on top and flip the jars upside down. Allow the jam to cool completely before turning right-side up.

If you want to process the jams - place them into a large pot, cover the jars with water by at least 2 inches and bring to a boil. Boil for 10 minutes, remove the jars and sit to cool.

Quince Jam

Makes 5-6 11 oz jars

Ingredients:

4 lb quinces

5 cups sugar

2 cups water

1 tsp lemon zest

3 tbsp lemon juice

Directions:

Combine water and sugar in a deep, thick-bottomed saucepan and bring it to the boil. Simmer, stirring until the sugar has completely dissolved. Rinse the quinces, cut in half, and discard the cores.

Grate the quinces, using a cheese grater or a blender to make it faster. Quince flesh tends to darken very quickly, so it is good to do this as fast as possible. Add the grated quinces to the sugar syrup and cook uncovered, stirring occasionally until the jam turns pink and thickens to desired consistency, about 40 minutes.

Drop a small amount of the jam on a plate and wait a minute to see if it has thickened. If it has gelled enough, turn off the heat. If not, keep boiling and test every 2-3 minutes until ready. Two or three minutes before you remove the jam from the heat, add lemon juice and lemon zest and stir well.

Ladle in hot, sterilized jars and flip upside down.

About the Author

Vesela lives in Bulgaria with her family of six (including the Jack Russell Terrier). Her passion is going green in everyday life and she loves to prepare homemade cosmetic and beauty products for all her family and friends.

Vesela has been publishing her cookbooks for over a year now. If you want to see other healthy family recipes that she has published, together with some natural beauty books, you can check out her Author Page on Amazon.

25686857R00049

Printed in Poland
by Amazon Fulfillment
Poland Sp. z o.o., Wrocław